Introduction

You Did Not Fall Behind. The Ground Moved.

For decades, the path of a software developer was relatively predictable. Learn a language. Master a framework. Gain experience. Move up the ladder. Junior became senior. Senior became lead. Lead became architect or manager. The rules were not always fair, but they were mostly stable.

That stability is gone.

Artificial intelligence did not arrive as a new tool at the edge of the profession. It arrived at the center. It did not change what developers build. It changed how value is created and who captures it. This shift is not incremental. It is structural.

Many developers sense this, even if they cannot yet articulate it. Tasks that once required years of experience can now be performed by systems that generate, refactor, and reason about code in seconds. Entry level work is disappearing. Senior work is being compressed. The familiar career ladder is bending under pressure, and in some places, it is breaking entirely.

This book is not about the end of software development. Development is not dying. What is ending is the traditional model of progression. The idea that increasing technical depth alone will reliably translate into career growth no longer holds. The environment has changed too much for the old assumptions to survive.

Artificial intelligence should not be understood as another productivity tool like version control or cloud infrastructure. It functions more like labor. It absorbs effort. It collapses time. It amplifies judgment. The developers who benefit most from it are not the fastest typists or the most specialized framework experts. They are the ones who understand systems, tradeoffs, and outcomes.

That distinction matters more now than it ever has.

Senior and staff level developers occupy a unique position in this transition. Their experience compounds in the presence of AI. Their judgment becomes more valuable, not less. At the same time, the signals that once defined seniority are losing meaning. Titles, years of experience, and even technical breadth are no longer sufficient indicators of impact.

This creates both risk and opportunity.

Those who continue to optimize for the old ladder may find themselves stalled, confused, or quietly displaced. Those who recognize the new shape of the profession can reposition themselves quickly. The difference between these paths is not talent. It is understanding.

The goal of this book is to provide that understanding.

You will not find prompts to memorize or tools to chase. Those change too quickly to matter. Instead, this book focuses on the underlying shifts that are reshaping development careers. It explains why junior leverage is disappearing, why senior leverage is accelerating, and why business context has become inseparable from technical excellence.

Most importantly, it outlines a practical path forward.

This is a book for developers who want to remain relevant, effective, and respected in a field that is changing faster than its institutions. It assumes you already know how to build software. What it offers is a clearer picture of how to build a career when the rules you started with no longer apply.

You are not late. But standing still is no longer an option.

Chapter 1

The End of Just Being Good at Code

For most of the modern history of software development, technical skill was the primary currency of career advancement. Developers who could write cleaner code, solve harder problems, or master new frameworks faster than their peers were rewarded with responsibility, influence, and compensation. The equation was simple. Improve your technical ability and your career would follow.

That equation no longer holds.

This change is often misunderstood as a matter of tooling. New languages, new frameworks, and new platforms have always reshaped how developers work. Teams adapted, skills shifted, and the ladder remained intact. Artificial intelligence is different not because it introduces new abstractions, but because it changes who performs the work and how quickly it can be done.

Writing code is no longer the bottleneck.

Tasks that once differentiated strong developers are increasingly handled by systems that generate, refactor, and analyze code at a speed that far exceeds human capability. Translating requirements into syntax, once a scarce and valuable skill, is becoming abundant. As abundance increases, differentiation decreases.

This does not mean that good code no longer matters. It means that being good at code is no longer enough.

For many developers, this realization creates immediate discomfort. Technical mastery has always been a reliable source of identity and confidence. Code quality is visible. Skill is measurable. Improvement is tangible. When these signals weaken, it can feel as though the ground beneath the profession is shifting unpredictably.

The instinctive response is often to learn more. New tools. New frameworks. New techniques. This response makes sense in a world where skill accumulation reliably translated into leverage. In an AI mediated environment, however, this strategy begins to fail quietly. The more execution oriented the skill, the faster it depreciates.

In earlier eras, technical excellence reduced risk. Skilled developers were trusted to produce reliable systems with fewer defects and less oversight. That trust translated into autonomy and advancement. Today, AI absorbs much of that execution risk by handling routine and well understood work. The marginal value of individual technical precision shrinks as tools improve.

This shift alters how organizations perceive contribution.

When execution becomes cheap, correctness becomes expected rather than celebrated. High quality output is assumed. What stands out instead are decisions that prevent rework, reduce complexity, and align effort with outcomes. These contributions are harder to see and harder to measure, but they increasingly define real impact.

What grows in importance is decision making.

Modern development environments are saturated with possibility. AI can propose multiple implementations, architectures, and tradeoffs in moments. The challenge is no longer how to produce an answer, but how to choose the right one. That choice depends on context, constraints, and long term consequences rather than syntax or speed.

This is where the traditional ladder begins to fail.

The ladder rewarded depth through accumulation. More languages. More frameworks. More patterns. But depth without direction now leads to diminishing returns. Developers can invest years refining skills that AI can replicate instantly while neglecting the judgment that AI cannot supply.

This creates a subtle mismatch between effort and reward.

Developers continue to work hard, often harder than before, while advancement slows or stalls. Performance reviews remain positive. Output remains strong. Yet influence does not grow at the same rate. Without a clear explanation, this stagnation is often internalized as personal failure rather than recognized as a structural shift.

Judgment is built through experience, but not just technical experience. It comes from seeing systems fail, watching tradeoffs play out over time, and understanding how decisions ripple across teams and organizations. These forms of learning were once secondary. They are now central.

Crucially, judgment does not scale the same way execution does.

It cannot be automated easily. It cannot be compressed indefinitely. It is shaped by context and consequence. This makes it both more valuable and more difficult to evaluate. Organizations accustomed to measuring output struggle to recognize judgment until its absence becomes costly.

The developers who continue to advance are not always the most technically impressive in isolation. They are the ones who can evaluate options, anticipate failure modes, and align technical decisions with real world goals. Their value lies not just in execution, but in integration.

This shift creates discomfort because it removes familiar signals.

Code quality, algorithmic skill, and framework mastery are visible and measurable. Judgment is not. As organizations struggle to evaluate it, they often fall back on outdated metrics. Output is rewarded even when outcomes suffer. Careers stall despite strong performance.

Over time, this misalignment produces predictable consequences.

High performing developers feel undervalued. Teams accumulate complexity despite shipping quickly. Decision making centralizes informally around a small number of trusted individuals while formal structures lag behind. The gap between how work actually gets done and how it is evaluated grows wider.

Yet the direction is clear.

Being good at code is becoming table stakes. The differentiator is the ability to decide what code should exist at all, where it should live, and why it matters. Developers who make this transition remain essential. Those who do not risk becoming interchangeable with the tools they use.

This chapter marks the end of a comfortable illusion. Software development has not lost its value, but it has changed what it values. The rest of this book is about understanding that change and using it deliberately rather than resisting it.

The Code Was Correct

The pull request was already approved by the time Marcus opened it.

That was new.

A year ago, anything touching this service would have waited for him. He had written most of it originally. He knew where the sharp edges were. He knew which optimizations mattered and which ones only looked clever in benchmarks.

Now the diff was clean. Smaller than expected. Generated with AI, refined by a mid level engineer, reviewed by another.

It was correct.

Marcus scanned it twice anyway. Habit more than necessity. The tests passed. The performance characteristics were acceptable. The solution was not elegant, but it was good enough, and good enough arrived faster than perfect ever had.

He approved it without comment.

Later that afternoon, a design discussion appeared on his calendar. No code attached. Just a question about whether a new dependency should be introduced or avoided. The tradeoffs were subtle. The decision would shape how three teams worked for the next year.

The meeting lasted fifteen minutes.

Marcus spoke twice. Once to rule out an option that would create long term coupling. Once to suggest a constraint the AI generated proposal had not considered. The team adjusted course immediately.

No one mentioned his pull request count for the sprint.

At the end of the day, Marcus realized something uncomfortable and clarifying at the same time. He had written almost no code, and yet his fingerprints were everywhere. The system was simpler. The teams were aligned. The future was cleaner than it would have been otherwise.

He closed his laptop.

Being good at code had built his career. Knowing when code should exist at all was now what sustained it.

Chapter 2

AI Did Not Kill Developers. It Killed Junior Leverage.

The first visible fracture in the development career ladder does not appear at the top. It appears at the bottom.

For decades, junior roles existed because organizations needed human effort to perform work that was necessary but not yet high leverage. Writing basic endpoints, fixing small bugs, implementing well defined features, and translating specifications into code all required time and attention. Juniors supplied that labor while learning the craft.

That economic arrangement is breaking down.

Artificial intelligence now performs much of this work faster, cheaper, and with fewer coordination costs than a new hire. The tasks that once justified junior positions are increasingly handled by systems that require no onboarding, no mentoring, and no long term investment. This is not a reflection of junior capability. It is a shift in how entry level value is created.

Junior leverage is disappearing.

Leverage refers to the ratio between effort and impact. Historically, juniors offered positive leverage by taking work off the plates of senior developers. They required guidance, but the net effect was increased throughput. As AI systems assume more of that workload, the leverage equation changes. Seniors can often move faster by working directly with AI than by delegating to a less experienced teammate.

This creates a quiet but significant reordering of work.

Tasks that were once ideal learning opportunities now feel inefficient to assign. The time required to explain context, review output, and correct misunderstandings can exceed the time it takes for an experienced developer to solve the problem directly with AI assistance. What disappears is not the need for juniors, but the economic justification for traditional junior work.

This is where many conversations become confused.

Some interpret declining junior hiring as a temporary market fluctuation. Others see it as a failure of training or education. In reality, it is a predictable response to changing leverage. When the cost of coordination exceeds the value of output, roles shrink or vanish regardless of intent.

This has cascading effects across organizations.

Entry level hiring slows. Expectations rise. The bar for what qualifies as a junior role quietly moves upward. Organizations still advertise junior positions, but the work attached to them increasingly resembles intermediate responsibility. Juniors are expected to contribute immediately, navigate complex systems, and operate with minimal supervision.

The apprenticeship model that sustained the profession for decades begins to erode.

This is not because mentorship stopped mattering, but because its economic foundation weakened. Apprenticeship assumes that early inefficiency is offset by long term growth. When AI absorbs much of the work that once justified that inefficiency, organizations struggle to justify the investment.

At the same time, senior leverage increases.

AI does not eliminate the need for experienced developers. It amplifies them. Seniors know where to apply effort, which risks to avoid, and which problems are worth solving. Paired with AI, they can explore options, validate ideas, and deliver outcomes at a scale that was previously impractical.

This creates a widening gap.

As junior leverage declines and senior leverage accelerates, the distance between entry level and experienced roles grows. The ladder becomes steeper and narrower. Fewer people can climb it, and those who do advance more quickly once they are established.

This divergence often feels unfair.

Junior developers may feel locked out despite strong fundamentals. Seniors may feel stretched thin, carrying both execution and decision making responsibilities. Organizations may struggle to reconcile short term efficiency with long term talent sustainability.

Ignoring this tension carries risk.

The long term danger is not a shortage of developers. It is a shortage of experienced developers. When entry points disappear, future senior capacity erodes. Organizations that optimize solely for near term leverage may find themselves fragile years later, unable to replace judgment that was never cultivated.

For individual developers, the implications are immediate.

Early career developers must find ways to create leverage that AI cannot easily replicate. This often means developing problem framing skills earlier, gaining system level understanding sooner, and seeking exposure to real consequences rather than isolated tasks.

For senior developers, responsibility shifts as well.

As traditional apprenticeship paths weaken, seniors play a larger role in shaping how experience is transmitted. Mentorship becomes less about teaching syntax and more about teaching judgment. Less about how to build and more about why to build at all.

This requires intentional effort.

Organizations that recognize this shift experiment with new models. Structured exposure to decision making. Shadowing rather than delegation. Smaller cohorts with deeper responsibility. These approaches attempt to preserve the development of judgment even as execution is automated.

This chapter is not a declaration of loss. It is a diagnosis.

The disappearance of junior leverage reveals the direction of change. It explains why entry points narrow, why expectations rise, and why frustration grows at the bottom of the ladder. Understanding this dynamic is essential before examining how the ladder itself is breaking.

The next chapter explores that collapse directly, and why progression from junior to senior is becoming harder to sustain in its current form.

Not Really a Junior Role

Lena stared at the job posting longer than she meant to.

"Junior Software Engineer."
Five years ago, she would have been overqualified.

Now the requirements scrolled on and on. Familiar tools. Distributed systems. Production experience. Comfort operating independently. It sounded like a mid level role wearing a junior title.

She applied anyway.

Two weeks later, she was invited to interview. The first round was short. No whiteboard. No algorithm puzzles. They asked her to talk through how she would approach a problem she had never seen before. She answered carefully, narrating her thinking. The interviewer nodded, occasionally redirecting.

The second round was stranger.

They shared a prompt. An AI generated solution appeared almost instantly. They asked her what she would change. She hesitated, then pointed out something subtle. Not a bug. A future constraint. Something that would make the system harder to evolve.

That was enough to move her forward.

On the team, Lena noticed the pattern immediately. There were fewer people than she expected. No true entry level roles. Everyone owned something real. AI handled the scaffolding. Humans handled the consequences.

She learned quickly, but not the way developers used to.

No one taught her how to write a loop. They taught her how to reason about impact. Why a decision mattered. When speed was dangerous. When simplicity was worth defending.

She worked harder than she ever had, but the work felt different. Less repetition. More responsibility. Fewer safety nets.

At the end of her first month, her manager told her something quietly.

"We don't really hire juniors anymore," he said. "We hire people who can grow into judgment."

Lena nodded, unsure whether to feel relieved or afraid.

Probably both.

Chapter 3

The Career Ladder Is Breaking

The traditional development career ladder was built on a simple assumption. Experience accumulates linearly, responsibility increases gradually, and value rises predictably over time. Junior developers learn to execute. Senior developers learn to design. Leaders learn to coordinate. This model worked because the work itself scaled with human effort.

That ladder was not perfect, but it was legible.

A developer could understand where they were, what was expected next, and how to progress. Time spent learning, building, and refining skills generally translated into greater scope and influence. Even when advancement was slow or uneven, the direction was clear. The ladder provided a shared mental model for growth, both for individuals navigating their careers and for organizations structuring roles.

That assumption no longer holds.

Artificial intelligence breaks the relationship between effort and output that the ladder depended on. As AI absorbs execution work and compresses timelines, the distance between levels shrinks in some places and stretches in others. The difference between junior and senior output narrows. The difference between senior and staff output widens. The middle of the ladder becomes crowded while the bottom thins out.

This creates a subtle but destabilizing effect.

Developers who are competent and productive begin to feel stuck. Promotions slow. Titles inflate without corresponding authority. Scope expands without clarity. Many are told they are operating at the next level while being evaluated by criteria that no longer reflect how value is created. The ladder still exists on paper, but it no longer maps cleanly to reality.

This misalignment is often difficult to articulate.

On the surface, nothing appears broken. Teams ship. Performance reviews are positive. Career frameworks are updated with new language. Yet movement feels inconsistent and unpredictable. Advancement becomes harder to explain, both to those who receive it and to those who do not.

This is not a performance problem. It is a structural one.

Years of experience have become a weak signal. In an environment where tools change rapidly and AI can replicate many execution tasks instantly, tenure alone no longer predicts impact. Framework familiarity decays faster than it accumulates. Skills that once took years to develop can now be approximated in minutes.

Organizations struggle to adapt to this shift.

Many respond by tightening promotion criteria without redefining them. Others inflate titles to retain talent without increasing scope. Some compress roles, asking fewer people to do more without adjusting expectations or authority. These responses address symptoms rather than causes, creating the appearance of stability while deepening confusion.

The result is widespread frustration that feels personal but is not.

Developers internalize stalled progression as individual failure. They work harder. They learn more tools. They take on additional responsibilities. When advancement still does not follow, confidence erodes. Without a clear explanation, the only available conclusion is self doubt.

This dynamic is particularly corrosive because it punishes precisely the behaviors that once led to growth.

Effort increases while returns diminish. The ladder promises progress but delivers ambiguity. Over time, motivation shifts from ambition to preservation. Developers focus on protecting their position rather than expanding their impact.

In reality, the ladder itself is misaligned.

It was designed for a world where execution scaled with people. Where adding more developers reliably increased output. Where experience accumulated primarily through repetition. AI disrupts all of these assumptions. Execution no longer scales linearly. Repetition no longer guarantees learning. Output is no longer the best proxy for value.

The middle of the ladder absorbs the shock first.

Mid level developers are asked to operate with increasing autonomy while lacking formal authority. Senior titles lose consistency across organizations. Staff roles become more ambiguous and unevenly defined. The distinction between levels blurs just as expectations rise.

This produces a paradox.

Responsibility expands, but recognition lags. Developers are trusted with more consequential decisions while still being evaluated using metrics designed for execution heavy work. The ladder stretches unevenly, creating gaps that are difficult to cross and rungs that feel arbitrarily placed.

At the same time, entry points narrow.

As discussed in the previous chapter, junior leverage disappears first. Fewer entry level roles exist, and those that remain demand higher readiness. This reduces the inflow of new talent and increases competition for mid level positions. The ladder becomes steeper at the bottom and more congested above it.

This is how ladders break.

Not through collapse, but through distortion. The rungs still exist, but they are unevenly spaced. Some are too close together. Others are suddenly far apart. Climbing becomes confusing, exhausting, and unreliable.

Senior and staff level developers experience this differently.

At higher levels, value shifts away from personal execution and toward decision making, integration, and ownership. The ladder struggles to represent this change because it was built to measure output, not judgment. Titles and promotion frameworks lag behind how work is actually done.

This mismatch creates tension on both sides.

Organizations struggle to identify and reward high leverage contributors. Developers struggle to understand how to grow without clear signals. Trust erodes as advancement feels arbitrary rather than earned.

Over time, informal structures emerge to compensate.

Decision making concentrates around a small number of trusted individuals. Influence accrues without title. Authority exists without formal recognition. While this can keep organizations functioning, it also increases fragility and burnout when responsibility is not matched with support.

The ladder is not broken because developers failed to climb it. It is breaking because it was built for a different economy of work.

Progression does not disappear, but it changes shape. Growth becomes less about ascending predefined rungs and more about expanding scope, influence, and responsibility. Developers advance by owning harder problems, not by accumulating years or tools.

Recognizing this shift early matters.

Those who continue optimizing for the old ladder may feel increasingly misaligned with how decisions are made and value is recognized. Those who understand why the ladder is breaking can reposition themselves around the work that remains scarce.

The next chapter introduces the central idea that makes this shift fully legible. To understand where the ladder is going, it is necessary to understand what AI represents inside organizations. Not as software, but as labor.

The Rungs Were Still There

No one announced that the ladder had changed.

On paper, everything looked familiar. Job titles still existed. Promotion cycles still ran. Performance reviews still asked the same questions. But inside the organization, something subtle had shifted.

Priya noticed it during calibration.

She had been recommended for promotion twice in two years. Each time, the feedback was positive. Strong contributor. Trusted. Consistent impact. And each time, the decision landed in the same place. Not yet.

The reasons were always reasonable. The scope was not quite broad enough. The influence was visible but hard to quantify. The criteria felt specific without being clear.

In meetings, newer hires deferred to her. Senior engineers asked for her opinion before committing to designs. Teams waited for her input before closing decisions. None of this appeared on the promotion rubric.

Meanwhile, others advanced.

Not because they made better decisions, but because their work fit the shape the ladder still expected. More visible output. More artifacts. More things that could be counted.

Priya began to understand the pattern.

The ladder had not collapsed. It had warped. The rungs were still there, but they no longer aligned with where the real weight was carried. Some were too close together. Others required a leap that no one could clearly explain.

She stopped chasing the next rung.

Instead, she focused on the work that pulled others toward her. Clarifying decisions. Reducing unnecessary complexity. Taking ownership of problems no one had formally assigned. Her influence grew quietly, even as her title remained the same.

Months later, when a new role was created to formalize responsibilities that already existed, no one debated whether she should take it.

The ladder had not moved for her.

The work had simply found a different way up.

Chapter 4

AI Is Labor, Not Software

Most technological shifts in software development have been framed as improvements to tooling. New languages increased expressiveness. Frameworks reduced boilerplate. Cloud platforms removed infrastructure constraints. Each wave changed how developers worked, but none fundamentally altered the relationship between effort and output.

Artificial intelligence does.

The most common mistake organizations make when thinking about AI is treating it like another tool in the stack. Something to adopt, integrate, and optimize around. This framing understates its impact and leads to poor decisions. AI does not simply improve productivity. It replaces large amounts of human effort.

AI behaves like labor.

This distinction matters because labor changes economics, not just workflows. When labor becomes cheaper and more abundant, timelines compress. When timelines compress, coordination and decision making become the dominant constraints. This is why the effects of AI feel disorienting even to experienced developers. The system dynamics have changed.

In traditional development environments, effort was scarce.

Writing code, testing it, reviewing it, and iterating all consumed time and attention. Many architectural and process decisions existed primarily to manage that scarcity. Tradeoffs were shaped by how much human effort could be applied safely, predictably, and sustainably.

AI removes much of that friction.

Code can be generated, revised, and explored rapidly. Alternatives that once required days of effort can be evaluated in minutes. Exploration becomes cheap. Revision becomes trivial. This abundance shifts the bottleneck away from production and toward selection.

The challenge is no longer how to build something.

It is what to build, when to build it, and whether it should exist at all.

This is where the labor model becomes clear.

AI does not replace developers in the same way automation replaced factory workers. It replaces slices of effort across the development lifecycle. It absorbs routine execution. It accelerates exploration. It reduces the marginal cost of trying another approach.

This redistribution of effort reshapes incentives.

When effort is expensive, caution dominates. Teams debate extensively before committing. When effort is cheap, experimentation increases. This can be healthy, but it also introduces new risks. Without strong judgment, abundance turns into noise. Teams can generate far more work than they can meaningfully evaluate.

The implication is subtle but powerful.

When effort is cheap, mistakes become cheaper to make, but also cheaper to correct. This encourages speed, but it also masks poor decision making. Systems may appear productive while quietly accumulating complexity. Progress can feel rapid even as direction degrades.

This is why AI amplifies differences rather than flattening them.

Developers who understand systems, constraints, and outcomes use AI to explore intelligently. They ask better questions. They discard weak options early. They recognize when speed creates risk rather than value. Developers without this context generate volume without direction.

The gap widens quickly.

Understanding AI as labor also explains why its impact is not temporary.

Labor saving technologies do not roll back. Once effort becomes cheap, organizations restructure around that reality. Roles change. Expectations shift. New forms of leverage emerge. Even if specific tools evolve or are replaced, the underlying economics remain.

This is not a trend cycle.

It is a reorganization of work.

Historically, when labor became more efficient, professions moved up the value chain. Accountants shifted from bookkeeping to advisory roles. Manufacturing workers moved from assembly to quality control and process design. Software development is following the same pattern, but at a much faster pace.

The danger lies in misinterpreting the change.

Organizations that treat AI as a productivity boost often double down on output metrics. Lines of code. Story points. Features shipped. These metrics become less meaningful when effort is abundant. What matters instead is outcome quality, decision coherence, and long term maintainability.

This misinterpretation creates a familiar failure mode.

Teams appear highly productive while accumulating hidden costs. Coordination overhead grows. Systems become harder to change. Technical debt increases not because work was rushed, but because decisions were made without sufficient context or restraint.

Developers feel this shift acutely.

Many sense that working harder no longer guarantees progress. Producing more code does not necessarily lead to more influence. In some cases, it leads to less. The developers who slow down to evaluate, simplify, and remove unnecessary work often deliver more value than those who accelerate blindly.

This inversion is uncomfortable because it contradicts long held instincts.

AI as labor also clarifies why judgment becomes the central skill.

Labor does not decide. It executes. AI can generate options, but it cannot own consequences. It does not feel the cost of rework. It does not experience outages, customer frustration, or organizational friction. That responsibility remains human.

As execution costs drop, the cost of poor judgment rises.

Small decisions compound faster. Mistakes propagate more widely. Direction matters more because velocity is no longer the limiting factor. In this environment, judgment becomes the scarce resource that determines whether abundance creates value or waste.

This is the foundation for the rest of the book.

Once AI is understood as labor, the collapse of the traditional ladder makes sense. Junior leverage declines because routine effort is automated. Senior leverage increases because decision making becomes more valuable. Roles reorganize around responsibility rather than output.

The next chapter examines how this reorganization changes the day to day shape of developer work. Specifically, how the profession is moving away from pure building and toward integration as the dominant source of leverage.

The Work Was Never the Hard Part

The team shipped three features that week.

All three worked. Tests passed. Metrics ticked upward. The sprint closed early, and the dashboard looked better than it had in months.

No one celebrated.

Alex noticed it during the retrospective. The room was quiet, not relieved. The conversation drifted away from delivery and toward questions that felt heavier than usual.

Why did we build this one first?
What problem were we actually trying to solve?
Which of these will we still want in six months?

The answers were uncertain.

AI had made the work easier than anyone expected. Prototypes appeared in hours. Variations were cheap. Rewrites were trivial. What used to feel expensive now felt disposable.

The problem was not effort.

The problem was deciding where effort belonged.

Later that day, Alex deleted more code than he wrote. Entire branches disappeared. A feature that had taken a day to generate was removed in minutes. It had never been wrong. It had simply never mattered.

No one objected.

The realization came slowly and then all at once. The hard part of the job had moved. Writing code was no longer the constraint. Choosing not to was.

AI did not make the team faster.

It made them responsible for something they had been able to ignore before. Direction. Coherence. Consequence.

As Alex closed his editor, he understood why the job felt different now.

The work was never the hard part.

Owning the outcome always was.

Chapter 5

From Builder to Integrator

For most developers, career growth has traditionally meant becoming a better builder. Writing cleaner code. Designing more robust systems. Delivering features more efficiently. Even as responsibilities expanded, the core identity remained tied to personal execution.

That identity is changing.

As AI absorbs more execution work, the highest leverage contribution is no longer producing code in isolation. It is integrating systems, decisions, and constraints into coherent outcomes. The developers who create the most value today are often those who write less code, not more.

This shift is easy to misunderstand.

Writing less code can look like disengagement. It can feel like a loss of relevance, especially in cultures where visibility is tied to artifacts and output. Many developers experience a quiet anxiety when their commit count drops, even if their influence increases.

Integration has always existed in development work, but it was rarely named or rewarded explicitly.

It lived between roles. Architects coordinated designs. Leads aligned teams. Senior engineers translated intent into implementation. This work mattered, but it was often treated as overhead rather than contribution. AI shifts integration from the margins to the center by making execution abundant and coordination comparatively expensive.

An integrator operates across boundaries.

This includes technical boundaries between systems and services, organizational boundaries between teams, and conceptual boundaries between product, business, and engineering. The integrator's value lies in reducing friction, avoiding misalignment, and ensuring that effort compounds rather than cancels itself out.

In a world where execution is abundant, misalignment becomes the dominant source of waste.

AI enables teams to generate multiple viable implementations in hours. Each option may be correct in isolation. Without integration, teams select approaches that optimize for local simplicity while creating long term complexity elsewhere. The cost does not appear immediately. It emerges over time as coordination overhead, brittle dependencies, and constrained future change.

Integrators prevent this outcome by asking different questions.

They focus on how choices interact with existing systems, how they affect future work, and how they align with organizational priorities. They consider not just whether something can be built, but whether it should be built now, in this way, by this team.

This form of contribution often lacks clean attribution.

When integration is done well, nothing dramatic happens. There are fewer reversals. Fewer emergency fixes. Fewer explanations required. The absence of problems becomes the signal, which makes the work difficult to see and easy to undervalue.

This shift requires a different skill set.

Builders optimize correctness and efficiency within defined boundaries. Integrators optimize coherence across boundaries. They must understand multiple domains well enough to make tradeoffs, even if they are not the deepest expert in any single one.

This can feel threatening.

Many developers equate expertise with depth. Integration, by contrast, values breadth and judgment. It rewards the ability to say no, to remove work, and to delay decisions until they can be made well. These instincts often run counter to cultures that celebrate speed and output.

AI reinforces the integrator role by lowering the cost of exploration.

When generating options is cheap, the value moves to evaluation and synthesis. Integrators use AI to surface possibilities quickly, then apply judgment to narrow the field. They are comfortable discarding work because they understand that progress is not measured by volume.

This changes how contribution feels.

Writing less code can feel like contributing less, even when impact increases. Integrators may appear less busy while quietly preventing expensive mistakes. Organizations that rely heavily on activity based metrics often struggle to recognize this value until its absence creates visible problems.

Over time, however, integration becomes impossible to ignore.

Systems remain simpler. Decisions stick. Teams move with fewer interruptions. Strategic initiatives align instead of competing. These outcomes accumulate into organizational effectiveness, even if no single moment can be pointed to as decisive.

The transition from builder to integrator is not a promotion.

It is a reframing of where value is created. Developers do not stop building. They build selectively. They focus effort where it shapes direction rather than where it merely produces output. AI handles routine execution, freeing attention for decisions that compound.

This transition is most visible at senior and staff levels, but it is not limited to titles.

Developers at any level who begin thinking in terms of integration rather than output position themselves for long term relevance. They become the people others consult before committing, not because they control resources, but because they reduce risk.

The next chapter addresses a misconception that often obscures this shift.

Many assume that success in AI assisted development depends on mastering prompts or tools. In reality, the differentiator is not how instructions are written, but how decisions are made.

Nothing Was Built, and Everything Changed

The document had started as a simple comparison.

Three approaches. Three diagrams. Three sets of tradeoffs generated with AI in under an hour. Any of them could work. All of them had supporters.

The meeting was supposed to decide which one to build.

Instead, it stalled.

Not because the options were weak, but because each one solved a different version of the problem. The room slowly realized they were not choosing an implementation. They were choosing a future.

Daniel had not spoken yet.

He had written very little code that quarter. His commit history looked thin. He had felt the quiet anxiety that came with it, the sense that visibility was slipping. Still, he had spent weeks listening. Watching where teams tripped over each other. Noting which systems required constant explanation.

He finally spoke, not to recommend an option, but to point out an overlap no one had noticed. Two teams were solving adjacent problems with different assumptions. Either approach would work in isolation. Together, they would fight each other.

Silence followed.

Then the conversation shifted. The diagrams were revised. One option disappeared entirely. Another was simplified. The third was deferred.

By the end of the meeting, there was less to build than when it started.

No tickets were created for Daniel. No tasks were assigned. Nothing concrete could be attributed to him in the sprint plan.

And yet, weeks later, when the work shipped smoothly and no unexpected coordination issues emerged, the team felt lighter. Decisions stuck. No one had to undo anything.

Daniel updated nothing on his resume.

But the system moved forward without friction.

Chapter 6

Prompting Is Not the Skill. Judgment Is.

As AI entered mainstream development workflows, attention quickly settled on prompting. How instructions are phrased. How context is supplied. How outputs are steered. This focus is understandable. Prompting is visible, concrete, and easy to discuss.

It is also misleading.

Prompting feels like a skill because it produces immediate, observable results. Better prompts often lead to better outputs. The feedback loop is fast. Improvement feels tangible. This creates the impression that mastery of prompting equates to mastery of AI assisted development.

That impression does not hold for long.

Prompting improves the surface quality of responses. Judgment determines whether those responses are worth using at all. As AI systems improve, the gap between a decent prompt and a great one narrows. The gap between a good decision and a bad one widens.

This distinction becomes clear in practice.

AI systems can generate many plausible solutions to the same problem. They can refactor code in multiple styles, propose different architectures, and suggest alternative tradeoffs. The outputs often look competent. Some are even impressive. The challenge is not generating options. It is deciding which option aligns with reality.

That decision depends on context.

Judgment draws on an understanding of constraints that AI does not own. Production behavior. Organizational priorities. Regulatory requirements. Team capacity. Long term maintenance costs. These factors are rarely fully captured in prompts, and even when they are mentioned, they require interpretation rather than execution.

Prompting produces candidates. Judgment selects outcomes.

This separation is easy to miss early on.

When AI is new, improvements in prompting produce dramatic gains. Developers feel empowered. Productivity spikes. Over time, however, these gains plateau. Most prompts become good enough. Differences in phrasing matter less than differences in evaluation.

At that point, prompting stops being a differentiator.

Judgment does not.

Judgment is not just knowing what looks right. It is knowing what will hold up. Experienced developers recognize this intuitively. They have seen systems fail in ways that were not obvious at design time. They have watched small decisions cascade into large problems. They understand that technical correctness does not guarantee operational success.

AI does not remove this complexity.

It amplifies it.

As generation becomes cheap, the cost of choosing poorly increases. Teams can explore more options than ever before, but exploration without discernment creates noise. Velocity without direction produces churn rather than progress.

This is where many organizations struggle.

They invest heavily in tooling and training around prompt quality while underinvesting in decision making capability. The result is a flood of output paired with growing uncertainty about direction. Teams move quickly but reverse often. Systems evolve rapidly but incoherently.

The failure is not technical.

It is evaluative.

Judgment also resists codification.

Best practices help, but they cannot replace lived experience. Many of the constraints that matter most emerge only under stress. Incidents. Scale. Real users. Organizational change. AI does not experience these conditions. Developers do.

This makes judgment difficult to measure and easy to overlook.

Organizations accustomed to tracking output struggle to assess decision quality until its absence becomes expensive. Only after outages, rework, or strategic misalignment does the cost of poor judgment become visible.

By then, the damage is already done.

This dynamic explains why prompting expertise alone rarely translates into influence.

Developers who can generate impressive outputs but cannot evaluate them accurately tend to stall. Their work looks productive, but it does not reduce uncertainty or risk. Over time, trust accumulates around those who consistently make sound decisions, even if their visible output is lower.

This can feel counterintuitive.

Developers are trained to demonstrate value through artifacts. Prompting produces artifacts quickly. Judgment often removes them. It cancels work. It delays action. It simplifies rather than expands.

These behaviors do not look like progress in activity based systems.

They look like restraint.

AI assisted development rewards restraint.

The ability to stop, question, and discard is more valuable than the ability to generate endlessly. Judgment determines when to use AI aggressively and when to ignore it entirely. It determines when speed helps and when it harms.

This is why judgment compounds.

Each good decision reduces future complexity. Each avoided mistake preserves optionality. Over time, developers known for sound judgment are trusted with broader scope. Their influence grows not because they control tools, but because they reduce risk.

Prompting will continue to matter.

But it will matter less than many expect. As models improve, prompt quality converges. Decision quality does not. The enduring differentiator will be the ability to evaluate outcomes in context and own the consequences of those evaluations.

This is the skill AI cannot replace.

The next chapter examines how this dynamic accelerates divergence among experienced developers. As judgment becomes central, those who possess it begin to pull away, reshaping teams and organizations in the process.

The Prompt Looked Perfect

The prompt had been refined carefully.

Clear instructions. Relevant context. Explicit constraints. It produced exactly what it was supposed to. The solution was clean, well structured, and confident. Anyone reviewing it in isolation would have approved it immediately.

Maya did not.

She stared at the output longer than necessary, trying to articulate what felt off. There were no obvious bugs. No missing cases. No performance red flags. The code was, by all conventional measures, good.

Still, she hesitated.

It assumed something that had never been written down. A deployment pattern the team had moved away from. A scale characteristic that only held during peak traffic. A convenience that would become a liability once real users arrived.

None of that appeared in the prompt.

It could not have.

Maya rewrote nothing. She discarded the solution entirely and asked the AI to explore a different direction, one constrained by realities learned the hard way. The next output was less elegant. More defensive. Slower to read.

It was the right one.

Later, a teammate asked why she had thrown away such a clean result. She struggled to explain. The reasoning lived in experience, not syntax. In incidents remembered. In tradeoffs paid for years earlier.

The prompt had been perfect.

It just did not know what mattered.

Maya committed the second version and moved on, aware that nothing about the interaction would be visible to anyone else.

Judgment rarely is.

Chapter 7

Why Senior Developers Are About to Pull Away

Experience has always mattered in software development, but its impact was often uneven. A senior developer might be faster or more reliable than a junior one, but the difference in output was usually bounded by time and attention. Everyone worked within roughly the same constraints.

AI removes many of those constraints.

When execution becomes cheap, experience compounds rather than plateaus. Senior developers are able to apply judgment across a much wider surface area, and AI amplifies that ability by reducing the cost of exploration and validation. The result is not incremental improvement. It is divergence.

Senior developers do not just move faster. They move with more intent.

They recognize patterns early and discard weak options quickly. They know which problems are worth solving and which are distractions. When presented with multiple AI generated solutions, they can evaluate tradeoffs almost immediately, not because the answers are obvious, but because they have seen the consequences of similar decisions before.

This ability to filter is critical.

AI generates abundance. Abundance without filtering creates noise. Junior developers often struggle here, not because they lack intelligence, but because they lack consequence history. They may generate many plausible options but lack the context to prioritize them. Seniors reduce complexity by saying no. They narrow scope. They simplify systems. These decisions save more time than any increase in typing speed ever could.

This filtering effect compounds across teams.

A senior developer paired with AI can explore design space rapidly, test assumptions cheaply, and converge on viable solutions with fewer iterations. Risks are identified earlier. Fragile paths are avoided before they are built. Over time, this leads to systems that are easier to change and teams that operate with less friction.

This is why senior leverage is increasing.

The gap between senior and junior contribution widens not because juniors are less capable, but because the environment rewards judgment over execution. AI narrows the execution gap while widening the judgment gap. Experience becomes a force multiplier rather than a marginal advantage.

Staff and principal roles benefit most from this dynamic.

These roles are defined less by direct output and more by influence over decisions. As AI accelerates execution, the value of shaping direction increases. Staff level developers operate across teams, align initiatives, and resolve ambiguity. AI allows them to test ideas quickly, but their primary contribution remains decision quality.

This changes how teams feel to work on.

Decisions stick longer. Reversals decrease. Momentum builds without constant correction. Teams led by high judgment contributors often appear calmer, not because they work less, but because they avoid unnecessary churn.

Organizations that recognize this shift restructure around it.

They reduce layers of coordination. They give senior developers broader scope. They rely on fewer people to make higher quality decisions. This leads to leaner teams with greater autonomy and faster alignment. These organizations often appear slower at first, but they compound faster over time.

Organizations that fail to adapt experience a different outcome.

High leverage developers become constrained by outdated role definitions. Decision making bottlenecks form around formal authority rather than judgment. Frustration increases as experienced contributors feel underutilized or ignored. Attrition rises quietly, often among those least easily replaced.

For individual senior developers, this moment presents a choice.

Some will continue to optimize for execution, competing with tools that are improving rapidly. Others will lean into decision making, integration, and responsibility. The latter group will pull away, not by working more, but by working at a different level.

This divergence is not hypothetical.

It is already visible in how teams operate, how influence is distributed, and how trust is earned. The developers who adapt early gain disproportionate leverage. Those who delay may find the gap increasingly difficult to close later.

This shift also alters peer dynamics.

Senior developers accustomed to parity may suddenly find large differences in influence and scope emerging among colleagues with similar tenure. These differences can be uncomfortable, especially when they are not reflected in titles or compensation immediately.

Over time, however, the pattern stabilizes.

Judgment accumulates trust. Trust expands scope. Scope amplifies impact. The compounding effect becomes unmistakable. Senior developers who operate at this level become central to organizational stability, even if their role descriptions lag behind reality.

The next chapter examines another dimension of this divergence.

As judgment becomes central, understanding how value is created outside of code becomes essential. Technical excellence alone is no longer sufficient. Business context increasingly determines where influence resides.

He Was Already in the Room

No one had officially invited Noah to the conversation.

The meeting was scheduled as a leadership sync. Product, design, engineering management. No individual contributors listed. Noah joined anyway, muted, camera off, listening while finishing another task.

The discussion moved quickly. Too quickly.

Options were presented. AI generated projections. Timelines collapsed into weeks instead of quarters. Everything sounded efficient. Everything sounded plausible.

Something felt wrong.

Noah unmuted once.

He did not challenge the direction. He asked a single question about an assumption buried in the rollout plan, one that depended on behavior that had never held under real load. The room slowed. Someone checked a metric. Another pulled up an incident from the previous year.

The plan changed.

After the meeting, no one mentioned Noah's title. No one referenced his output for the sprint. But later that day, three people messaged him independently, asking for his thoughts before finalizing related decisions.

He noticed the pattern had become consistent.

He was not the fastest developer anymore. He wrote less code than he used to. But his calendar filled with moments where things could go wrong if no one intervened.

AI made it easier for others to move fast.

Experience made it easier for him to know when not to.

He had not been promoted recently. His role description had not changed. But more decisions passed through him than ever before.

He was already in the room.

Chapter 8

Business Context Is the New Technical Depth

For much of the history of software development, technical depth was the primary differentiator. Developers who understood systems deeply, mastered complex frameworks, or optimized performance at low levels were rewarded with influence and responsibility. Business considerations were often treated as external constraints rather than core inputs.

That separation no longer holds.

As AI reduces the cost of execution, the relative value of technical depth changes. It remains important, but it no longer operates in isolation. The developers who have the greatest impact are those who understand how technical decisions connect to business outcomes.

Business context does not replace technical expertise. It directs it.

Understanding how value flows through an organization allows developers to focus effort where it matters most. This includes knowing which metrics drive decisions, which constraints are fixed, and which tradeoffs are acceptable. Without this context, even well engineered solutions can miss the mark.

This shift is often uncomfortable.

Many developers were trained to treat business concerns as distractions. Deadlines were seen as arbitrary. Metrics were viewed skeptically. Product decisions felt political rather than principled. In a slower environment, this distance was survivable. In an AI mediated one, it becomes costly.

AI amplifies this dynamic.

When generating solutions is easy, the risk shifts from underbuilding to misbuilding. Teams can deliver technically sound systems that fail to produce meaningful outcomes. Developers who understand business context are better positioned to prevent this by aligning technical work with real priorities.

Consider how this shows up in practice.

AI enables rapid development of new features. From a purely technical perspective, shipping more functionality seems beneficial. But without understanding customer behavior, revenue models, operational costs, or regulatory exposure, these features may increase complexity without increasing value. Maintenance burdens grow. Focus diffuses. The organization becomes harder to steer.

Developers with business context ask different questions.

They evaluate whether a feature addresses a real problem, whether it aligns with strategic goals, and whether it justifies its long term cost. They recognize that sometimes the highest leverage decision is not to build, but to simplify or remove.

This form of judgment often lacks immediate feedback.

A technically impressive solution that misses business intent may still ship successfully. Its failure emerges slowly, through adoption gaps, support burden, or strategic drift. Conversely, a decision not to build rarely produces visible celebration, even when it prevents long term harm.

This makes business context easy to undervalue.

At senior and staff levels, however, its absence becomes impossible to ignore.

As developers gain influence, their decisions shape not just codebases but organizations. Choices about architecture, tooling, and prioritization affect team velocity, hiring, and adaptability. Without business context, these decisions risk optimizing for local efficiency at the expense of global outcomes.

This is where many technically strong teams falter.

They build elegant systems that are misaligned with how the organization creates value. They optimize performance where users do not notice. They invest in flexibility where stability is needed. AI accelerates these mistakes by making it easier to act quickly without pausing to ask why.

Business literacy changes communication.

Developers who can articulate technical tradeoffs in terms of value, risk, and opportunity are more likely to be trusted with broader scope. They translate engineering concerns into business language and business goals into technical constraints. This translation role becomes more valuable as AI accelerates technical work and increases the pace of decision making.

This does not mean abandoning rigor.

In fact, business context sharpens technical judgment. It clarifies which problems are worth solving deeply and which optimizations are premature. It helps developers choose when to invest in resilience and when to accept risk. Technical depth becomes more selective, not less.

Some developers resist this shift.

They worry that business considerations dilute technical integrity or compromise quality. In practice, the opposite is true. Without business context, technical rigor often becomes misdirected. With it, rigor is applied where it matters most.

Over time, this changes how influence is earned.

Developers known for understanding the business become central to planning and decision making. Their input is sought earlier. Their recommendations carry more weight. This influence is rarely tied to formal authority at first, but it compounds as decisions consistently lead to better outcomes.

AI accelerates this compounding.

As execution becomes faster, the cost of misalignment rises. Organizations increasingly rely on those who can connect technical possibilities to business realities. Business context becomes the new form of depth, not because it replaces technical skill, but because it determines where that skill creates value.

The next chapter turns inward.

As some skills compound and others decay rapidly, developers must decide how to invest their own learning. Choosing what to learn and what to stop learning becomes a strategic decision rather than a personal preference.

The Question Behind the Question

The request came in as a technical task.

A feature expansion. Reasonable scope. Clear acceptance criteria. The kind of work that would have been celebrated for moving quickly just a year earlier. AI had already produced a working version by the time the ticket was assigned.

Rachel paused before approving it.

Instead of asking how long it would take, she asked why it existed.

The answer was vague. Competitive parity. Customer demand. A metric that had dipped slightly the previous quarter. None of it was wrong. None of it was convincing.

She scheduled a short call.

In ten minutes, the shape of the problem changed. The feature addressed a symptom, not the cause. It added complexity where clarity was needed. It would improve a dashboard without improving a decision.

The work was canceled.

No code shipped. No sprint points were earned. The backlog got smaller instead of larger.

Later, a product leader thanked her, not for saving time, but for reframing the conversation. The team redirected effort toward a simpler change that reduced churn without adding surface area.

Rachel returned to her desk and declined three more tickets that week.

Each time, she explained the reasoning in terms the business understood. Cost. Risk. Focus. Opportunity.

Her technical depth had not changed.

But it was no longer the thing people relied on most.

They came to her because she asked the question behind the request.

Chapter 9

What to Learn and What to Stop Learning

In periods of rapid change, learning feels like the safest response. New tools emerge. New frameworks gain attention. New techniques promise relevance. For many developers, the instinct is to absorb as much as possible in the hope that breadth will protect them.

That instinct is understandable.

For most of the profession's history, learning more reliably led to greater opportunity. New skills unlocked new projects. New tools increased leverage. The risk of learning the wrong thing was relatively low because skills aged slowly and effort compounded predictably.

That environment no longer exists.

AI changes not only how work is done, but how skills age. Some skills compound over time, becoming more valuable as experience accumulates. Others decay quickly, losing relevance as tools evolve and automation advances. The challenge is no longer learning faster. It is learning selectively.

Not all learning creates leverage.

Execution focused skills tied to specific tools, libraries, or syntactic patterns now depreciate more rapidly than before. AI systems can replicate these capabilities quickly and consistently. Mastery in these areas may still be useful in the short term, but it no longer guarantees long term advantage.

This creates a subtle trap.

Learning feels productive even when it produces diminishing returns. Developers can spend significant time mastering a tool that will soon be abstracted away or replaced. The effort is real. The payoff is temporary. When relevance fades, the sense of loss can feel disproportionate to the investment.

Compounding skills behave differently.

Systems thinking improves with exposure. The ability to reason about tradeoffs strengthens as more decisions are made and evaluated. Communication skills deepen as developers navigate more complex organizational environments. Domain understanding grows as consequences are observed over time. These skills retain value even as tools change.

The difference is durability.

A useful test is to ask whether a skill would still matter if the tooling around it changed completely. If the answer is no, the skill is likely decaying. If the answer is yes, it is probably compounding. This distinction helps clarify where time and attention should be invested.

This does not mean avoiding technical learning.

Technical skills remain necessary, but they must be chosen with intent. Learning a new language or framework should expand the kinds of problems a developer can reason about, not just the speed at which familiar problems are solved. The goal is to increase scope, not efficiency alone.

AI complicates this decision.

AI lowers the cost of experimentation, making it easier to explore unfamiliar areas. Developers can prototype quickly, test assumptions, and gain exposure without deep upfront investment. Used well, this accelerates learning. Used poorly, it encourages shallow accumulation without understanding.

This is where judgment reappears.

Choosing what to learn is now a strategic decision. Time spent mastering a narrowly scoped tool may feel safe, but it often produces diminishing returns. Time spent developing judgment, communication, and system awareness compounds even when specific technologies fade.

This shift can feel uncomfortable.

Many developers derive identity and confidence from technical mastery. Letting go of constant tool acquisition can feel like stagnation or decline. In reality, it creates space for deeper growth. It allows developers to focus on understanding problems rather than collecting techniques.

There is also a social dimension.

Communities often reward novelty. Conference talks, blog posts, and online discussions gravitate toward new tools and techniques. Durable skills are harder to showcase. Their impact is subtle and long term. This can distort perception, making decaying skills appear more valuable than they are.

For senior and staff developers, this distinction is critical.

At higher levels, value is created less through individual execution and more through influence over decisions. Skills that support this influence become increasingly important. Writing clearly. Framing problems. Evaluating tradeoffs. Mentoring others. These abilities scale impact beyond personal output.

Stopping certain forms of learning is part of this transition.

This does not mean disengaging from the profession. It means recognizing when additional depth in a specific tool no longer produces meaningful leverage. It means choosing not to chase every trend, even when doing so feels risky.

Over time, this selectivity becomes liberating.

Learning shifts from accumulation to refinement. Developers become clearer about what they are optimizing for and why. Their growth becomes less reactive and more intentional.

The most effective learning plans today are not aggressive.

They are deliberate. They balance technical refresh with sustained investment in durable skills. They treat AI as a partner in exploration, not a substitute for understanding. They prioritize clarity over coverage.

The next chapter examines how these learning choices translate into career progression.

As the ladder changes shape, developers need a new model for growth, one that reflects how leverage is now created rather than how it once was.

The Shelf Kept Getting Longer

Owen noticed it while reorganizing his bookmarks.

The list of tools he had meant to learn kept growing. New frameworks. New AI workflows. New languages that promised relevance. Each one came with articles, tutorials, and confident predictions about the future.

He added another tab.

Later that week, he was asked to review a proposal. The technical solution was sound. Modern. Well researched. It used tools Owen had only skimmed. Still, something felt fragile about it.

Not wrong. Fragile.

He traced the assumptions instead of the implementation. What would break first. What would be hardest to change. What depended on conditions that rarely held for long. None of this required knowing the tool deeply. It required knowing how systems aged.

He left comments sparingly.

The proposal was revised. Simplified. Some of the newer pieces were removed entirely. The final version was less impressive on paper and more durable in practice.

Afterward, Owen closed half his bookmarks.

He did not feel behind. He felt lighter.

The shelf of things he understood deeply had not grown quickly, but it had grown in the right direction. Fewer items. More weight.

The future, he realized, would not reward knowing the most things.

It would reward knowing which things lasted.

Chapter 10

The AI Augmented Career Path

As the traditional career ladder loses clarity, many developers search for a new set of rules to replace it. Titles no longer map cleanly to responsibility. Years of experience no longer guarantee progression. The question becomes less about how to climb and more about how to move.

This uncertainty is deeply uncomfortable.

The ladder provided predictability. Even when advancement was slow, it was legible. Developers could orient themselves around known milestones and expectations. As that structure erodes, many experience a sense of drift, unsure how to measure progress or evaluate tradeoffs.

The emerging path is not linear.

It is scope driven.

In an AI mediated environment, careers advance through expanding responsibility rather than ascending predefined rungs. Developers grow by taking ownership of broader, more ambiguous problems and by making decisions that shape outcomes beyond their immediate codebase.

This reframes what progression looks like in practice.

Early in a career, progress is often measured by execution. Can a developer deliver features reliably? Can they work independently? As AI absorbs more of this execution, advancement depends increasingly on judgment and integration. The next step is not doing more of the same work faster. It is taking responsibility for harder problems.

Scope becomes the primary signal.

Scope includes the size of problems a developer can handle, the number of stakeholders they can align, and the complexity of systems they can reason about. Expanding scope means moving from implementing solutions to defining them, from owning tasks to owning outcomes.

This transition is often uneven.

Developers may take on more responsibility before recognition follows. They may operate at a higher level without a title change. This lag can be frustrating, especially for those accustomed to clear milestones. Yet it is a predictable feature of scope driven growth rather than a failure of the individual.

AI supports this transition by reducing the cost of entry into new domains.

Developers can use AI to explore unfamiliar areas quickly, build prototypes, and validate ideas without deep initial expertise. This lowers the barrier to taking on broader responsibilities. It also raises expectations. When exploration is cheap, the ability to act on insights becomes the differentiator.

This creates a new form of pressure.

It is no longer enough to understand one system deeply. High leverage developers must reason across systems, teams, and constraints. AI makes this possible, but it does not make it easy. The cognitive load shifts from execution to synthesis.

The AI augmented career path rewards those who seek ambiguity.

Rather than waiting for clear instructions, high leverage developers identify gaps, frame problems, and propose solutions. They use AI to test assumptions and refine approaches, but they retain ownership of decisions. This willingness to operate without complete information becomes a defining trait of senior influence.

This represents a significant shift in mindset.

In the past, ambiguity was often avoided. Clear requirements were seen as a prerequisite for success. Today, ambiguity is where leverage lives. Those who can navigate it calmly and responsibly become central to organizational progress.

This path also changes how growth is demonstrated.

Traditional markers such as promotions, certifications, or visible output matter less than sustained impact. Developers advance by showing that their decisions reduce risk, simplify systems, and enable others to move faster. These contributions accumulate quietly, often without immediate recognition.

Organizations respond to this behavior, even when formal structures lag behind.

Developers who consistently expand scope are trusted with more responsibility. They become go to decision makers. Their influence grows informally before it is recognized formally. This is often how staff and principal roles emerge in practice, regardless of title.

This informal growth can feel risky.

Without clear milestones, developers may worry they are drifting rather than advancing. This anxiety is understandable, but it reflects a mismatch between old expectations and new dynamics. Scope driven careers require trust in compounding impact rather than immediate validation.

The AI augmented career path is not about abandoning technical excellence.

It is about applying it selectively. Developers still need strong technical foundations, but they use them to evaluate options rather than to prove competence. They choose when to dive deep and when to remain at a higher level. AI assists with execution, freeing attention for strategy and integration.

This selectivity becomes a form of discipline.

Not every problem deserves deep technical investment. Not every system needs to be optimized. Judgment determines where depth creates value and where it creates drag.

Over time, this discipline produces resilience.

Careers built around expanding scope rather than accumulating credentials adapt more easily to change. As tools evolve, the ability to frame problems, align stakeholders, and make sound decisions remains valuable.

The AI augmented career path lacks a checklist.

There is no universal sequence of steps. Progress is measured through trust, influence, and the ability to handle complexity. This ambiguity can be uncomfortable, especially for developers accustomed to concrete goals. Over time, however, it produces careers that are more durable and less dependent on specific technologies.

The next chapter examines how this shift affects hiring.

As organizations adapt to AI mediated work, the signals they use to evaluate developers are changing. Understanding these signals is critical for positioning yourself effectively in the years ahead.

No One Gave Him the Role

The work started small.

A question no one owned. A decision deferred too many times. A gap between teams that kept reappearing in different forms. No ticket described it clearly. No role was responsible for fixing it.

So Aaron did.

At first, it was just conversations. Clarifying intent. Aligning assumptions. Using AI to explore options quickly so discussions could move forward instead of looping. He made no announcements. He asked no permission.

People noticed anyway.

They began to wait for his input before finalizing plans. They forwarded him threads that felt messy. They trusted him with ambiguity because he seemed comfortable inside it.

His title did not change.

His calendar did.

When performance reviews came around, his manager struggled to summarize his impact. There were fewer artifacts than expected. Fewer features directly attributed to him. But the organization moved more smoothly in places he touched.

A few months later, leadership formalized a role that looked suspiciously like the work Aaron was already doing. He was offered it without applying.

No one had given him the role.

He had simply started operating at that level.

Chapter 11

How Hiring Will Change by 2030

Hiring has always lagged reality in software development, but the gap has widened significantly in the age of AI. Job descriptions still emphasize familiar signals. Years of experience. Specific technologies. Past titles. These markers once correlated reasonably well with future performance.

They no longer do.

As AI reshapes how work is done, the signals that predict impact change faster than hiring frameworks can adapt. Organizations continue to screen for execution oriented indicators even as execution becomes less scarce. The result is a growing mismatch between who is hired and who creates the most value.

Traditional hiring optimized for output potential.

Resumes were evaluated for evidence of productivity. Shipped features. Known frameworks. Recognizable companies. Interviews tested problem solving under artificial constraints, often favoring speed and recall. These approaches worked when individual execution capacity was the primary limiter of progress.

AI changes that equation.

When execution is cheap, the ability to produce code is no longer the primary differentiator. What matters instead is the ability to make sound decisions in complex environments. Hiring processes built around output signals struggle to detect this capability.

This creates two parallel failures.

Organizations miss candidates with high judgment but unconventional backgrounds. At the same time, they overvalue candidates who present well under execution heavy interview formats but struggle when asked to operate with ambiguity and responsibility.

These failures are rarely obvious at first.

New hires may perform well in the early stages of onboarding. Tasks are well defined. Scope is narrow. AI assists with ramp up. Over time, however, cracks appear. Decisions are escalated unnecessarily. Complexity accumulates. Teams slow down despite high activity.

Judgment reveals itself gradually.

It becomes visible in how developers frame problems, not just how they solve them. In how they identify risks early rather than reacting to them. In how they simplify systems rather than expanding them unnecessarily. These qualities are difficult to surface in traditional interviews.

This is why hiring is becoming more probabilistic.

Organizations increasingly rely on extended evaluation. Trial projects. Probationary periods. Informal references. Signals accumulate over time rather than appearing in a single interview loop. While imperfect, this reflects an acknowledgment that judgment cannot be reliably assessed through short exercises.

Job descriptions struggle to keep up.

Many still list extensive technical requirements that no longer map cleanly to day to day work. Candidates are asked to demonstrate mastery of tools they may rarely use directly. Meanwhile, critical expectations around decision making, communication, and integration remain implicit.

This implicitness creates confusion.

Candidates optimize for what is written, not for what actually matters. They prepare for algorithmic interviews while underpreparing for real world ambiguity. Organizations hire for familiarity and then wonder why adaptation is slow.

AI further complicates evaluation.

Candidates can now produce impressive artifacts quickly. Code samples. Take home assignments. Architectural diagrams. These materials may look strong, but they increasingly reflect AI assisted execution rather than individual judgment. Without careful interpretation, hiring teams risk conflating polish with capability.

This does not mean artifacts are useless.

It means they must be contextualized. How a candidate explains tradeoffs. What they choose not to build. How they reason about constraints. These discussions reveal more than the artifact itself.

Over time, some organizations adapt.

They shift interviews toward scenario based discussions. They explore how candidates think through messy problems. They evaluate communication and alignment skills alongside technical competence. These changes are uneven, but the direction is clear.

For candidates, the implications are subtle but important.

Optimizing solely for resume keywords and technical drills produces diminishing returns. Demonstrating judgment, clarity, and the ability to operate responsibly under uncertainty becomes increasingly valuable, even if it is harder to signal explicitly.

This transition can feel frustrating.

Strong candidates may be overlooked by outdated processes. Others may be hired despite misalignment. Over time, however, organizations that fail to adapt pay a cost in churn, rework, and stalled momentum.

Hiring signals will continue to evolve.

As AI mediated work becomes the norm, organizations will refine how they identify high leverage contributors. The process will remain imperfect, but it will increasingly favor those who reduce uncertainty rather than those who merely produce output.

The final chapter turns from organizational dynamics to individual agency.

With signals shifting and structures lagging, developers must decide how to position themselves deliberately over the next phase of their careers. The question is no longer how to be selected, but how to remain valuable as conditions continue to change.

The Interview Was Different This Time

The interview did not start with a coding problem.

That was the first thing Elias noticed.

No shared editor. No algorithm. No request to invert a tree or reason about time complexity. Instead, the interviewer shared a short document describing a system that had grown organically over several years.

"Walk me through what you would do next," she said.

Elias paused longer than he used to. In the past, he would have started diagramming immediately. Identifying components. Proposing improvements. Showing momentum.

Instead, he asked a question.

"What problem are you trying to solve right now," he said, "and which ones can wait?"

The interviewer smiled slightly and answered honestly. The system was stable but brittle. Teams were stepping on each other. Everyone could ship, but no one felt confident about the direction.

Elias talked through tradeoffs rather than solutions. He described paths he would avoid. Decisions he would delay. Risks he would surface early so they could be owned explicitly rather than discovered later.

At one point, the interviewer asked him to use AI to explore alternatives.

He did, briefly. Then he closed it.

“This is where I’d stop,” he said. “Anything beyond this would look productive but increase uncertainty.”

The room was quiet for a moment.

After the call, Elias realized something had shifted. He had not tried to prove he was smart. He had tried to show how he thought. He had not competed with the tool. He had used it and then stepped past it.

When the offer arrived, it was for a role that did not quite match any title he had held before. The description focused on responsibility, not output. Influence, not velocity.

Elias accepted without negotiating the title.

For the first time in a long while, the interview had felt like a conversation about reality rather than a test of endurance.

Chapter 12

Your 24 Month Survival and Advantage Plan

Every profession has a moment when its inherited assumptions stop working. The work may look similar on the surface, but the forces shaping it have changed. For software development, that moment is arriving now.

The phrase "traditional developer" does not describe a lack of skill or intelligence.

It describes a set of expectations formed in a different economic reality. A world where execution scaled with people. Where experience accumulated predictably. Where mastery of tools reliably translated into advancement. These assumptions shaped how developers learned, how organizations hired, and how careers progressed.

That world is fading.

AI does not eliminate software development, but it dissolves the conditions that made the traditional model stable. Execution becomes abundant. Exploration accelerates. Decision making becomes the bottleneck. The profession reorganizes around judgment rather than output.

This creates a generational boundary.

Developers who built their careers entirely within the old model often feel disoriented. The signals they relied on weaken. The strategies that once worked produce diminishing returns. Effort no longer correlates cleanly with progress.

This disorientation is not a failure.

It is a mismatch between expectation and reality.

The last generation of traditional developers is not defined by age, but by orientation. They are the final group trained to believe that being excellent at execution was sufficient. That belief was reasonable when the environment rewarded it. It becomes limiting when the environment no longer does.

What replaces it is not a single new archetype.

There is no standardized role that neatly fills the gap. Instead, the profession fragments along lines of judgment, responsibility, and scope. Developers differentiate themselves not by what they can build, but by what they choose to own.

This shift can feel destabilizing because it removes certainty.

There is no longer a guaranteed path from competence to advancement. Progress depends on context. Influence depends on trust. Growth depends on willingness to engage with ambiguity rather than avoid it.

Many will resist this change.

Some will continue to optimize for execution, hoping that excellence alone will reassert its value. Others will disengage, interpreting the shift as a loss of fairness or clarity. These responses are understandable, but they do not alter the underlying dynamics.

The profession moves regardless.

At the same time, new developers enter under different assumptions.

They grow up with AI as a baseline. They treat generation as normal. Their differentiation emerges earlier around judgment, framing, and integration. They do not experience the same loss because they never relied on the old guarantees.

This creates tension across experience levels.

Veteran developers possess deep intuition and context but may struggle to reposition their value. Newer developers adapt quickly but lack consequence history. Organizations must navigate this transition carefully or risk losing both.

The most resilient developers bridge these worlds.

They carry forward the discipline, rigor, and responsibility forged under scarcity while adapting to abundance. They recognize that execution skill still matters, but only as a foundation. They invest in judgment because it compounds even as tools change.

This is the quiet opportunity within the disruption.

The collapse of the traditional ladder does not mean the end of meaningful careers. It means the end of automatic ones. Growth becomes intentional. Influence becomes earned through trust rather than time. Value becomes visible through outcomes rather than activity.

This requires a shift in identity.

Developers must stop defining themselves solely by what they produce and start defining themselves by the problems they solve and the decisions they own. This transition is uncomfortable because it cannot be completed through study alone. It requires exposure, responsibility, and reflection.

AI accelerates this reckoning.

By removing execution as the primary differentiator, it forces clarity. It reveals where judgment exists and where it does not. It exposes misalignment quickly. It rewards those who can integrate, decide, and simplify.

The last generation of traditional developers stands at a choice point.

Not between relevance and irrelevance, but between adaptation and friction. Those who adapt early reposition themselves around durable leverage. Those who do not may continue to work hard while feeling increasingly out of sync with how value is recognized.

This book has not argued for abandoning the craft.

It has argued for understanding where the craft now lives.

Software development remains a profession of thinking, responsibility, and consequence. Code is still written. Systems are still built. But the center of gravity has shifted. The future belongs to developers who recognize that shift and respond deliberately.

The traditional developer is not disappearing.

They are becoming something else.

And the developers who understand this transformation are not witnessing the end of their profession. They are participating in its redefinition.

Conclusion

You Are Not Late. But Standing Still Is No Longer an Option.

There is a temptation, at moments like this, to search for certainty.

To ask which skills will matter, which roles will survive, and which paths will remain safe. That instinct is understandable. For most of its history, software development rewarded predictability. The ladder existed because the future looked enough like the past to extrapolate from it.

That is no longer true.

The discomfort many developers feel today is not rooted in fear of obsolescence. It is rooted in the loss of guarantees. The profession no longer promises that effort will be repaid on a fixed schedule, or that competence alone will be noticed, or that time served will naturally convert into authority.

This loss feels personal, but it is structural.

What AI has removed is not the need for developers, but the illusion that value can be measured mechanically. When execution becomes abundant, clarity becomes scarce. When tools accelerate work, judgment determines whether acceleration leads somewhere useful.

This forces a reckoning.

Developers must decide whether they want to be evaluated by activity or by impact. Whether they are willing to own decisions rather than tasks.

Whether they are comfortable being accountable for outcomes that cannot be fully predicted in advance.

These questions do not have universal answers.

Some will choose stability over scope. Some will prefer clearly bounded roles even as their influence narrows. Others will lean into ambiguity, accepting uncertainty in exchange for relevance and trust. Neither choice is inherently wrong. But pretending the choice does not exist creates frustration.

The profession will stratify around this distinction.

Not cleanly. Not immediately. But steadily. Developers who take responsibility for direction will accumulate influence, often quietly at first. Those who optimize for execution alone will find their work increasingly mediated, constrained, or commoditized.

This is not a moral judgment.

It is an economic one.

AI has changed the cost structure of work. When something becomes cheap, it stops defining value. When something becomes scarce, it becomes decisive. Today, what is scarce is not code, but judgment under uncertainty.

That scarcity reshapes everything.

How teams are staffed. How trust is earned. How leadership emerges. How careers progress. The visible artifacts of development remain, but the invisible work grows in importance. The conversations before code is written matter more than the code itself.

This is why the transition feels subtle but relentless.

Nothing breaks overnight. No single tool causes collapse. Instead, small mismatches accumulate. Promotions stall. Influence shifts. Titles lose meaning. Developers sense that something fundamental has changed but struggle to articulate what it is.

This book has attempted to name that change.

Not to predict the future in detail, but to clarify the forces already in motion. To explain why familiar strategies feel less effective. To reframe AI not as a competitor, but as a reallocation of labor that exposes where human contribution truly lies.

The last generation of traditional developers is not being left behind.

They are being asked to evolve without a map.

Those who succeed will not do so by chasing tools or mastering prompts. They will succeed by becoming reliable decision makers in an environment where decisions matter more than ever. They will be trusted not because they are fast, but because they are careful. Not because they produce the most, but because they waste the least.

This kind of value is harder to demonstrate.

It requires patience. It requires restraint. It often goes uncelebrated until it is absent. But over time, it becomes unmistakable. Organizations stabilize around it. Teams depend on it. Systems reflect it.

The future of software development is not automated.

It is clarified.

AI strips away the noise and forces the profession to confront what it has always been about beneath the abstractions. Responsibility. Judgment. Consequence. The developers who embrace that reality are not watching the end of their careers.

They are shaping what comes next.

And in that sense, being part of the last generation of traditional developers is not a disadvantage. It is a vantage point.

You have seen both worlds.

What you do with that perspective is what will matter most.

www.ingramcontent.com/pod-product-compliance
Lightning Source LLC
La Vergne TN
LVHW022023200926
848481LV00007B/2515